KRAKÓW

AND SURROUNDINGS

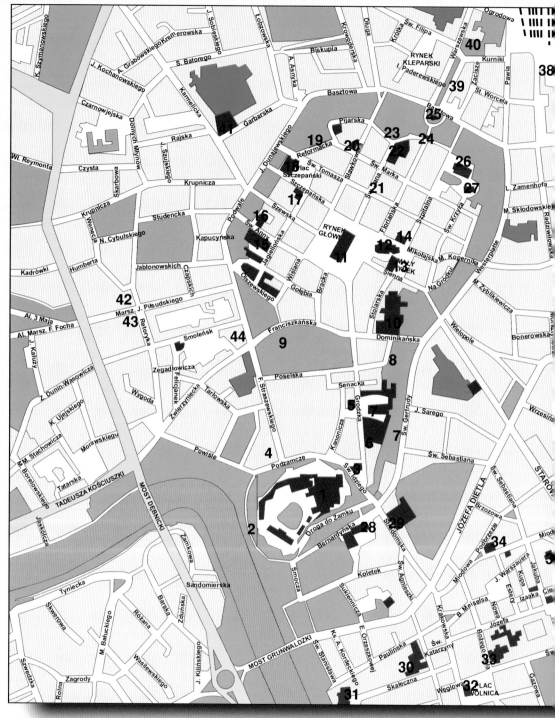

1. Wawel
2. Wawel's Dragon
3. St Aegidius Church
4. The Deanery
5. Collegium Iuridicum
6. St Andrew's Church
7. Church of SS Peter and Paul
8. St Joseph's Church
9. Franciscan Church
10. Dominican Church
11. Drapers' Hall

12. St Mary's Church
13. St Barbara's Church
14. Monsignor's residence of St Mary's Church
15. Collegium Maius
16. Church of St Anne
17. Stary Theatre
18. Palace of Arts
19. Church of the Reformati
20. Church of St Mark the Evangelist
21. Church of St John
22. Czartoryski Museum.

23. Church of the Piarist Fathers
24. Floriańska Gate
25. Barbican.
26. Julisuz Słowacki Theatre
27. Holy Cross Church
28. Bernardine Church
29. Missionary Priests Church
30. St Catherine's Church
31. Church at Skałka
32. Kazimierz town hall
33. Corpus Christi parish Church

Photography by: Stanisława, Jolanta and Rafał Jabłoński

Text by Rafał Jabłoński

Graphic design by Rafał Jabłoński

Cover photo: St Mary's Church
Back cover photo: Wawel Cathedral

Print: Perfekt, Warszawa

The photographs in this album are from the Jabłoński Family Archives.
Telephone: +48 (22) 642-06-71; cellphone: 06024422992;
website: www.jablonski-archiwum.neostrada.pl

ISBN 83-920325-2-7

FESTINA Publishers, tel/fax (22) 842-54-53
e-mail: festina@neostrada.pl, website: www.festina.republika.pl
Copyright FESTINA Publishers

WARSAW 2005

KRAKÓW

The beginnings of Kraków are buried in time. According to legend, the founder of the city was Prince Krak who defeated a terrifying dragon living in a cave at the foot of Wawel Hill. Upon the advice of the cobbler Skuba, he stuffed a calf skin with sulphur and placed it at the mouth of the dragon's cave. The dragon, thinking it to be a savoury tit-

Kraków Christmas crèche contest.

bit, gobbled it up only to feel the sulphur burning his innards. To douse the burning the dragon drank and drank from the Vistula until finally he burst. According to tradition, a relic of those times is Krak's mound, containing the grave of Kraków's first ruler. The historic beginnings of the settlement on the banks of the Vistula are connected to the emergence of the Polish state. A fortified town standing guard over nearby settlements of the Vistulian tribe grew up on Wawel Hill in the 9th century.

Towards the end of the 9th century, it formed its own state constituting a part of the Great Moravian State and subsequently Bohemia. Most likely in 977, the Polanian Prince Mieszko I conquered the lands inhabited by the Vistulians and established his rule over them in 981. After his death, his son Boleslaus the Brave ascended to the Wawel throne. The consolidation of lands carried out by that ruler led to the emergence of a Polish state in the full sense of the term. At that time, Kraków moved into the

View of Kraków from 'Civitas orbis terrarum', 1603-c.1605. Fragment.

forefront of the state's other capitals. Towards the end of the 10th century it became an episcopal see subordinated to the archbishopric of Gniezno. That set Kraków apart from other European cities. The grandson of Boleslaus the Brave, Kazimierz the Renewer, acknowledged Kraków as the capital of his realm. It was also the seat of his successor, Boleslaus the Bold who in 1079 murdered Bishop Stanislaus of Szczepanów, for which he was banished from the land. He was followed on the throne by Ladislaus Herman, who only briefly transferred his ducal seat to Płock. Even then, Kraków remained Poland's intellectual centre.

On Wawel Hill, next to the cathedral founded by Boleslaus the Brave and several smaller Romanesque rotundas, a small ducal castle was built. Round the foot of Wawel Hill a settlement known as Okół began arising. Together with adjacent localities it intensive-ly developed in a northerly direction. In the 12th century there were dozens of churches in Kraków, an impressive number by European standards. It was most likely during the reign of Duke Leszek the White, in the first half of the 13th century, that the town received its first charter that designated its central market place in the vicinity of St Andrew's Church. That legal act, however, was only a prelude to the great charter granted in 1257 by Duke Boleslaus the Shy. After the town had been plundered and set ablaze in a Tartar invasion in 1241, it became necessary to map out broader limits for its redevelopment. Not only Wawel, but also St Andrew's Church was destroyed. The new charter in effect laid out a new town which did not however include Okół and many other existing settlements such as the later Kazimierz or Zwierzyniec.

The central market square, one of the biggest in Europe, was surrounded by a regular network of streets. Soon the construction of ramparts got under way, and subsequently town walls studded with 47 watchtowers were built. Since the town was established in accordance with German-style legal norms, it attracted German settlers from Silesia, where such norms had been adopted the earliest. The German population's eventual numerical advantage over that of native Poles led to frequent conflicts. During the reign of Duke Ladislaus the Short, in 1312 a revolt led by Alderman Albert, leader of the city's German community, erupted in support of Bohemian rule over Kraków. Violently suppressed, it contributed to closer ties between Kraków and the rest of Poland. The German language was expunged from municipal records and replaced by Latin. During the coronation of King Ladislaus in 1320, Wawel Cathedral was officially declared the coronation site of Polish kings, a privilege that was to remain in force until the mid-18th century. Wawel cathedral also became the final resting place of King Ladislaus in 1333. From then on, the cathedral became the burial site of Poland's monarchs. Wawel Cathedral, which acquired its present Gothic form at that time, became time, became for

Poles a repository of national mementoes.

Following the death of King Ladislaus the Short, King Casimir the Great ascended the throne. It was he who brought about the country's full stability and made a major contribution to the development of its capital. The new towns of Kazimierz and Kleparz arose within Kraków's orbit of influence and eventually became town districts. Many monumental Gothic structures were built such as St Mary's Church, St Catherine's Church and Corpus Christi Church in Kazimierz. Beyond Kraków, defensive strongholds were erected in Ojców, Lanckorona and Skawina. In 1364, with papal consent, Casimir the Great established an academy of learning in Kraków, Central Europe's second university after that of Prague (1348).

Poland's ruling Piast Dynasty ended with the death of Casimir the Great in 1370. Following the brief rule of the Anjou Dynasty of Hungary, in 1286 a Polish-Lithuanian union was concluded with the marriage of the Princess Hedwig to Lithuanian Duke Jagiełło. The country's stabilisation following the Peace Treaty of Toruń, ending hostilities with the Teutonic Knights of the Cross, and the acquisition of the port of Gdańsk, affording Poland access to the Baltic Sea, contributed to the development of the state and its capital. Many outstanding structures were erected in Kraków such as the Drapers' Hall, the Barbican and Col-

legium Maius as well as many churches and monasteries.

The reign of the last two Jagiellonians—Sigismund the Old and Sigismund Augustus—has been regarded as Kraków's 'golden age'. Many splendid structures in the then new Renaissance style went up. Suffice it to mention King Sigismund's Chapel in Wawel Cathedral and the castle courtyard's arcaded galleries.

With the death of the last of the Jagiellonians, the city's days of glory became a thing of the past. King Stefan Batory and his wife Anna Jagiellonian rarely stayed in Kraków. The focus of public affairs gradually began shifting northwards to Warsaw. From 1596, that is where the Sejm (diet) of the Commonwealth convened. Sigismund III Vasa, who was related to Anna Jagiellonian, started the Swedish-derived Vasa Dynasty. While it is true that Sigismund III initially took up residence on Kraków's Wawel Hill, after the victorious

Battle of Smolensk in 1611, he returned to Warsaw Castle. Although officially it would remain the capital down to the very end of the dual Polish-Lithuanian Commonwealth, it gradually became a provincial city. It came alive only during funerals and coronations with their attendant coronation diets.

The dynastic policies of the Vasas led to a Swedish invasion known as the Deluge, which had tragic consequences for Poland and Kraków. In 1655, Sweden's King Carl X Gustaf occupied the lands of Poland and Lithuania. Despite the valiant efforts of Hetman Stefan Czarniecki, Kraków was incapable of resisting the siege. Apart from imposing huge levies, the Swedes plundered church treasuries and

Horse-drawn carriage in the Main Marketplace.

Kraków-style pretzels may be purchased on almost every street corner.

The time of reforms was interrupted by the pro-Russian Confederation of Targowica which brought about the second partition of Poland in 1793. The Russians captured Kraków and held it for two years up until an insurrection led by Tadeusz Kościuszko broke out. But the freedom did not last long. Following the Poles' victory in the Battle of Racławice. They were defeated at Szczekocin. The road to Kraków lay wide open and after a brief battle the city was captured by the Prussians. In 1795, the third and final partition of Poland took place, and Kraków became part of Austria. The same year, the Prussians robbed Wawel Cathedral of the royal insignias and

A flock of pigeons in the Main Marketplace.

libraries. When King John Casimir entered the city in 1657, its houses were in ruins and the streets were littered with the bodies of those killed during the siege.

The death of Augustus III in 1763 marked the end of the reign of the Saxon Dynasty in Poland. In accordance with the will of Russia's Tsarina Catherine II, Stanislaus Augustus Poniatowski was elected king in a free election. That period as marked by economic, political and cultural reforms, but it was also a time of setbacks for the Commonwealth. A conflict between a portion of the gentry and the king weakened the state and led to the first partition of Poland in 1772, in which the southern part of Little Poland was annexed by Austria. Kraków became a border town of a Polish state truncated by the partitioning power. The Austrians did everything in their power to economically weaken a city that did not belong to them.

On the left bank of the Vistula, along to road leading to Wieliczka, they built the rival town of Podgórze. Economically privileged, it brought about the economic collapse of Kraków. King Stanislaus Augustus set about reforming the state. In 1775, a Good Order Commission was set up in Kraków to reform the city's institutions In 1775, Hugo Kołłątaj set about reorganising the Kraków Academy which was in a state of stagnation.

deliberately destroyed them. That was a symbolic gesture to deprive the Polish nation of statehood for all time.

Despite the lack of statehood, the Poles' drive for independence never died. It was Kraków that became a bastion of national identity. By accumulating various national mementoes connected with the nation's glorious past, it became a symbol of national unity. During the Napoleonic wars, Kraków was incorporated in the Duchy of Warsaw, which was meant to reactivate national existence. It lasted until Napoleon's defeat in 1813. In 1815, the Congress of Vienna established the Free City of Kraków, known as the Kraków Republic, subordinated politically to the partitioning powers. Many changes were introduced at that time. The city's mediaeval walls came down and a green belt was laid out in their place. The Kościuszko Mound was created to commemorate the heroic leader of an insurrection started in Kraków. During the 1831 Insurrection, which broke out in the Russian partition zone, Kraków supplied the insurgents with arms and later became the centre of all of Poland's conspiratorial movements. The authorities of the partitioning powers were well aware of that fact. In 1833, they concluded a secret agreement allowing them to occupy Kraków in the event of any insurgency. The Kraków Republic came to an end in 1864, when a revolution lasting nine days broke out in Kraków. The city was incorporated into Austria and its people suffered reprisals. Kraków would again become the centre of revolutionary activity in 1848 during the Springtime of Nations. The Austrians left Kraków and sought refuge in the Wawel. After a state of emergency was introduced, reprisals were renewed and Germanisation was stepped up.

A new turning point for Poland as well as Kraków was the year 1914, the start of the World War which would restore the country's independent statehood. Situated on the periphery of Poland, it continued to serve as a centre of culture and learning. That was also the case during the two between-the-wars decades. The Second World War brought with it a five-year occupation period marked by arrests, street roundups and forced labour in Hitler's Third Reich.

Cultural relics were plundered, including the Marian altar of Wit Stwosz. Kraków avoided all destruction during its liberation in 1945. The new social order was not accepted by most Kraków inhabitants. The city paid for its attitude by being consigned to a peripheral role. In 1947, the decision was taken to build alongside of Kraków a huge metallurgical complex, the Lenin Steelmill, which soon contributed to the ecological destruction of the city and its architectural relics. Thousand-year-old Kraków, one of Europe's most beautiful cities, in 1978 was included on UNESCO World Cultural Heritage list.

Flower vendors in the Main Marketplace.

WAWEL

The Wawel was the ancient stronghold of the Vistulians, a tribe that became part of the Polish state of Mieszko I. From the 9th century a densely built-up ducal seat was located there. From the reign of Boleslaus the Brave and Casimir the Renewer until the 17th century (when the state's capital was moved to Warsaw), the Wawel was the centre of state authority. In later centuries it was the scene of royal funerals and coronations.

» The originally the word 'wawel' meant an elevation within a swamp. The name reflects the location of the limestone hill's location amid the Vistula's marshy surroundings and flood waters.

≽ A stone statue of St Sigismund marks the Vasa Chapel at Wawel Cathedral.

⚒ The big Jurassic cave at the foot of Wawel Hill, gouged out ages ago by sea waves, is associated with the legendary dragon of King Krak's times. In front of the cave stands a sculpture of the dragon created in 1972 by Bronisław Chromy.

⚒ A view of the northern side of Wawel Cathedral and Castle.

⚒ A view of the eastern side of Wawel Castle and its fortifications.

» A monument to Tadeusz Kościuszko was erected in 1921 on the bastion of Ladislaus IV. It was the work of the Lwów sculptor Leonard Marconi, completed after his death by his son-in-law, Antoni Popiel.

⩾ The main entrance to the Wawel leads through the Gate of Crests, built in 1921 and adorned with the crests of lands once belonging to the Dual Polish-Lithuanian Commonwealth.

« Senator's Tower, once known as Lubranka, was erected in the mid-15th century during the reign of Casimir the Jagiellonian.

» Thieves' Tower was built at the Lower Castle during the reign of Casimir the Great in the mid-14th century.

≫ A southern view of Wawel Cathedral and vicarage. Visible in the square in front of the cathedral are the surviving foundations of the Wawel's mediaeval structures.

≫ Sandomierz Tower was erected before the middle of the 15th century.

≫ The initially Gothic vicarage was remodelled on two occasions: in 1522 and again in the latter half of the 19th century.

⌃ The Archcatehdral of SS Stanislaus Bishop and Martyr and Wenceslaus received its present shape in the 14th and 15th centuries. Construction of the first cathedral began after the year 1000.

« The bones of post-glacial animals over the cathedral entrance.

« The cathedral's interior is that of a three-nave basilica with cross-ribbed and palm vaulting.

≫ These early-Baroque pews dating from c. 1620 were the work of master cabinet-maker Jan Szabura.

≯ A row of royal crypts, starting with the Romanesque crypt of St Leonard, are found below the cathedral's main floor. This is a remnant of the second cathedral built during the reign of Ladislaus I Herman.

« The Confession of St Stanislaus, created in 1626-1629 according to the design of Giovanni Trevano, is situated at the point where the cathedral's main nave and transept intersect.

» In the years 1594-1595, Anna Jagiellonian ordered the creation of a tomb chapel for her husband, King Stefan Batory. The task was entrusted to Stani Gucci who also designed an impressive monument to the ruler.

≽ The tombstone of Ladislaus II Jagiełło (who died in 1434) was created during the king's lifetime in about 1420. The canopy was created in 1519-1524 by Giovanni Cini.

« The canopied tombstone of King Ladislaus of Varna was created in 1906 by Anotni Madejski.

≽ The sarcophagus of King John Olbracht is found in a niche constituting Poland's oldest Renaissance relic. It was created in 1502-1505 by Francesco of Florence.

≽ The canopied sarcophagus of King Casimir the Great was created in a Hungarian workshop after 1370.

≫ The sarcophagus of Queen Hedwig was made of Carrera marble in 1902 by Antoni Madeyski. The sculptor patterned himself on the 15th-century tombstone of Ilaria del Caretto in Lucca Cathedral.

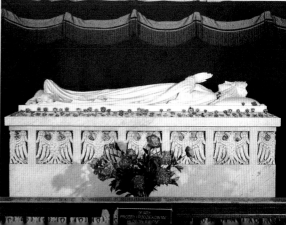

« Holy Cross Chapel was founded by King Casimir the Jagiellonian and his wife Elisabeth Rakuszanka. The vaulting and walls are adorned with polychromy created in about 1470 by painters from Pskov in Muscovy.

≽ King Sigismund's Chapel, Poland's most outstanding example of Italian Renaissance architecture, was created in the years 1519-1533 according to the design of Bartolomeo Berrecci.

≽ The tombstone of King Casimir the Jagiellonian in Holy Cross Chapel was created in 1492 by Wit Stwosz in co-operation with Jorg Huber of Passau.

≽ The Holy Trinity Triptych in Holy Cross Chapel dating from c. 1467.

⌃ The entrance to Wawel Royal Castle leads through a two-storey gatehouse.

⌐ This rectangular courtyard, surrounded by two-storey arcaded galleries, was built during the reign of King Sigismund I the Old. The castle's Renaissance-style renovation was begun directly after the ruler's coronation in 1507. The work was carried out by numerous artists including Francesco of Florence, Benedict of Sandomierz, Bartolomeo Berrecci and Matthew of Italy. The renovation was concluded before the mid-16h century.

« The polychromy adorning the second-storey gallery walls was the work of painter Dionizy Stuba.

« An exhibition entitled the Orient in the Wawel Collection has been set up on the first and second storeys of the castle's west wing. The core of the collection are the Oriental memorabilia, captured during the 1683 Battle of Vienna, including various military artefacts and Turkish banners. Also on display is an extensive collection of Oriental tents.

« The Hall of Deputies, situated on the second storey in the east wing, was where Poland's Sejm convened. A ceiling frieze from the latter half of the 16th century portrays the annals of human life, inspired by the text of the ancient Greek writer Kebes.

≫ The ceiling of the Hall of Deputies is adorned with coffers containing rather unique facsimiles of human heads, sculpted in the latter half of the 16th century by Jan Janda and Sebastian Tauerbach of Wrocław. Of the original 194 heads, only 30 have survived.

« Between the Hall of Senators and the Hall of Birds is a hallway richly decorated with a coffered ceiling.

⨠ The Baroque Hall of Birds on the north wing's second storey opens an enfilade of chambers appointed during the reign of the Vasa Dynasty.

⨠ The Battle of Orsza Hall.

» The Vasa bed chamber is situated in the Gothic Pavilion.

OKÓŁ

As early as the 9th century, a wooden settlement existed round the base of Wawel Hill along the Salt Route leading from Hungary to Great Poland. It has chiefly inhabited by craftsmen and the duke's cohorts. Originally a collection of wooden cottages surrounded by palisades, over the centuries it evolved into the town's elite quarter comprising grand palatial mansions and churches.

» Art Nouveau polychromy depicting Polish flowers—poppies, lilies, mulleins, dandelions et al—which adorns the Franciscan Church, was the work of Stanisław Wyspiański, a distinguished painter of the Modernist Period. The work was commissioned by the church's guardian, Father Samuel Raiss.

≫ The oldest surviving Kraków crest, 'Podelwie', dating from the 14th century, adorns the house at No. 32 Grodzka Street.

⌃ The wall of Długosz House at No. 25 Kanoniczna Street reveals a 1480 bas-relief depicting Jan Długosz as its founder.

⌃ The Gothic Church of St Aegidius was built at the start of the 14th century. In 1595, it became the property of the Dominicans who soon set about remodelling it.

⌃ The stalls at St Aegidius Church are a remnant of the late-Baroque tombstone of St Hyacinth moved there from the Dominican Church.

« The Royal Aresenal (No. 64 Grodzka Street) was built in the first half of the 16th century by King Sigismund I the Old.

» Kanoniczna Street was once the last stretch of the Royal Way leading to the Wawel.

« The house at No. 23 Kanoniczna Street was known as 'Lisia Jama' (Fox Den). A Baroque portrait of St Jonah, patron saint of lawyers, is found above the entrance portal.

≽ The Deanery (No. 21 Kanoniczna Street) was built in the latter half of the 14th century thanks to Canon John of Brzesko. In 1582-1592, the structure was remodelled with the participation of the outstanding architect and sculptor, Santi Gucci. He designed a portion of the galleries surrounding the building's internal courtyard.

≫ ≪ Collegium Iuridicum (No. 53 Grodzka Street) of the Kraków Academy was erected at the start of the 15th century thanks to the bequest of Queen Hedwig.

≪ Gothic elevation of the house at No. 8 Kanoniczna Street.

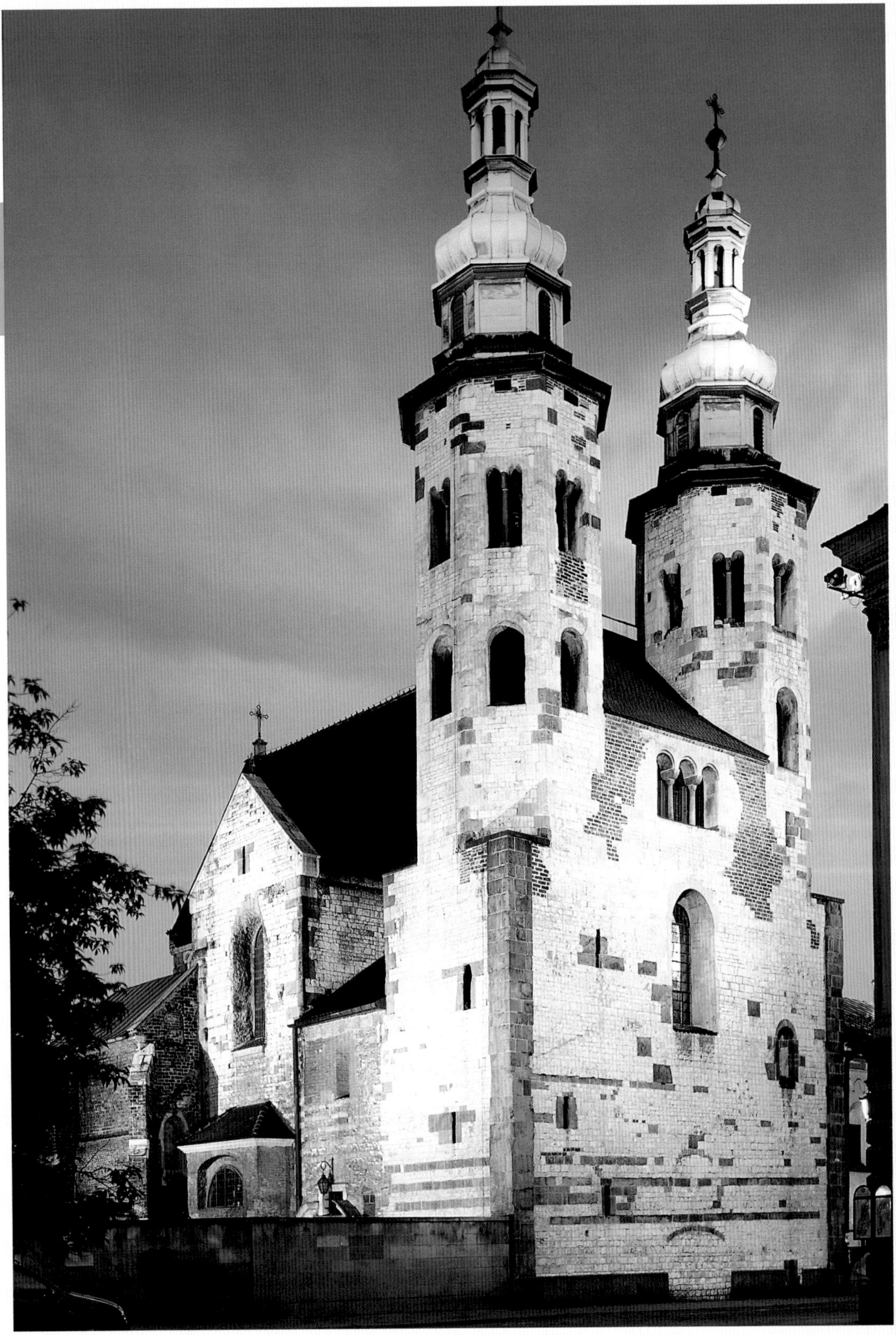

Founded by the powerful Sieciech, palatine of Duke Ladislaus Herman, St Andrew's Church was built in 1079-1098. In 1200, the church was enlarged and given its Romanesque defensive form. As a result, it was the only one to withstand the Tartar invasion of 1241. Its interior was remodelled in the Baroque style in around 1702.

≽ The Baroque tombstone of Bishop Andrzej Trzebnicki was enshrined in the Church of SS Peter and Paul in 1695-1696.

The early-Baroque Church of SS Peter and Paul was built in 1596-1605 according to the design of Giovanni de Rosus. Its form alludes to that of Rome's Il Gesù Church.

⩘ A crest depicting an elephant and rhinoceros adorns Elephant House.

« St Joseph's Church and the adjoining Bernardine Sisters' Convent were built in 1694-1704. The altars and pulpit were created in 1697 in the workshop of Kraków woodworker Jerzy Hankis.

⩘ A monument to Józef Dietl, a distinguished Kraków mayor, stands in All Saints Square.

« The town hall acquired its modernist appearance in 1907-1912.

≽» Thanks to the endowment of Duke Henryk the Pious, a church was built in 1241-1249 for the Franciscans brought to Kraków from Prague. In the first half of the 15th century the church was considerably enlarged and its presbytery was extended. Numerous remodelling projects, usually after fires, were carried out until 1912.

« The Franciscan Church owes its present appearance largely to the renovation that followed an 1850 fire and lasted until 1912. The church was endowed with neo-Romanesque and neo-Gothic features.

» The stained-glass window of Blessed Salome was the work of Stanisław Wyspiański.

⋗ The main nave's rich mural decorations were created in 1904 by painter Tadeusz Popiel.

«Neo-Gothic stalls were built between 1883 and 1891 under the supervision of Friar Konrad Preisner. The figures in the upper portion depicting scenes from the life of the Blessed Mother and St Francis were created in 1991.

« The chapel of the Sorrowful Madonna is situated at the right side of the main nave. It once constituted the fourth arm of the galleries.

⩒ These Gothic galleries were created in 1423-1455 thanks to the endowment of Cardinal Zbigniew Oleśnicki. Illuminated by sharply arched windows, they surrounded the quadrangular garth.

⩓ The Baroque Chapel of Our Lord's Passion, constituting part of the Gothic side nave, is situated on the left side of the main nave. It was remodelled in the Baroque style following a blaze in 1655.

⩓ The 17th-century sacristy appointments reflect the Baroque style. The polychromy dates from 1897.

« Stanisław Wyspiański's stained-glass window entitled God the Father is situated above the choir loft.

A CHARTED CITY AND PLANTY

In 1257, Duke Bolesaus the Shy gave Kraków its major town charter. Round the quadrangular marketplace measuring 200 x 200 metres he mapped out a geometric street grid of identically sized parcels. They were built up over the ages with increasingly opulent structures. By endowing the town with its own local government, law court and commercial privileges, the duke turned it into an independent legal entity.

» The Adam Mickiewicz Monument, Drapers' Hall and town-hall tower exemplify the coexistence of architectural relics from different epochs.

≽ The statue of a mediaeval Kraków student standing at the centre of St Mary's square is a copy of one of the figures in Wit Stwosz's famous carved altar.

» The Chapel of Our Lady of the Rosary was built in 1685-1688.

≽ On the north wall of the Dominican Church's presbytery is the plaque of Filip Kallimach, created according to the design of Wit Stwosz.

≫ Brought from Bologna in 1222, the Dominicans soon set about building their first church in Kraków. After it was destroyed in a fire in 1225, its reconstruction was begun in about 1250.

» The original appointments of the three-nave basilica were all but totally destroyed in a blaze, hence most of its objects date from the 19th century.

« Then mannerist tombstone of Wieliczka Salt Mine overseer Prosper Provana was created in about 1600.

≫ Monastery buildings adjoin the north side of the Dominican Church. Its garth is surrounded by Gothic galleries, whose 13th-century walls were covered over the centuries by the epitaphs of Kraków burghers.

« ≈ A wide staircase leads to the Chapel of St Hyacinth, which was renovated in the late-Baroque style by Baltazar Fontana in c. 1700.

≈ The neo-Gothic tombstone of General John Skrzynecki was created in 1865 by Ladislaus OleszczyńSki.

« Next to their monastery, the Dominicans built merchant stalls meant for hire in 1861.

« In this house (No. 16 Rynek), Nicholas Wierzynek gave a famous royal banquet in 1364 for the guests of King Casimir the Great.

⩘ Icon House (No. 19 Rynek), originally belonging to the Cellari Family, in 1718 it was decorated with an icon of the Blessed Virgin Mary.

⩘ » Hetman House (No. 17 Rynek), dating from the latter half of the 14th century, ranks among the oldest dwelling houses in Kraków. A chamber with Gothic vaulting and decorative keystones has survived in its cellars.

≈ The classicist façade of Potocki Palace (No. 20 Rynek) was created in 1777-1783.

≋ » Since 1956, Ram Palace (No. 27 Rynek) has been a home to the famous Ram Cellar Cabaret, originated by Piotr Skrzynecki. His bronze likeness graces his favourite café table.

⩘ Kraków's principal administrative building was its town hall, built at the turn of the 14th century. Frequently remodelled over the centuries, it was finally dismantled in 1817-1820.

⩔ St Adalbert's Church is Kraków's oldest place of worship. It is not unlikely that St Adalbert himself preached there before setting out on his missionary journey to Prussia.

⩘ » At the centre of the Kraków marketplace is a drapers' hall known as Sukiennice. The hall was built round merchants' stalls in the mid-14th century. Following a fire in 1555, the structure was rebuilt in the Renaissance style.

≫ Two rows of market stalls formed an inner alley, closed off by decorative grates to protect against theft.

≫ The first floor of the Drapers' Hall contains a Gallery of Polish Painting belonging to the National Museum. Above: Władysław Podkowiński's 'Madness of Excitement'.

⩕ A contemporary rendition of the 'Crucifixion' graces a niche in the apse of St Mary's Church.

⩘ The unveiling of Teodor Rygier's Adam Mickiewicz Monument took place in 1898. Tadeusz Stryjeński was the author of the entire architectural project.

» St Mary's Church was built as a parish church for Kraków burghers even before the town had been chartered. The original Romanesque church was remodelled in the Gothic style round the turn of the 14th century. The renovation project continued until 1446.

The most outstanding work of art in Kraków's old parish church is the Marian polyptych created by Wit Stwosz, a master woodcarver who moved to Kraków from, Nuremberg. He worked on the panelled altar with interruptions from 1477 to 1489.

» The Garden of Olives at St Barbara's Church.

≫ This superb Art Nouveau dwelling house (No. 4) at the corner of St Mary's Square and the Marketplace (Rynek) was commissioned by Celestyn Czynciel and built in 1908. Its author, Ludwik Wojtyczko, decorated the first floor with stuccowork displaying Mercury's staff.

» The Gothic Church of St Barbara was built in St Mary's Square in 1338-1402 thanks to Queen Hedwig's endowment. According to legend, the bricks used to build it were left over from the construction of St Mary's Church. Originally, St Barbara's Church was the graveyard chapel of St Mary's Cemetery. Later, it was taken over by the Jesuits who own it to this very day.

≫ A chapel dating from 1606 at St Barbara's Church.

≫ The monsignor's residence of St Mary's Church was erected in 1618-1619 by master builder Jan Zatorczyk.

⩕ ⩔ Collegium Novum was erected according to Feliks Księżarski's design in 1883-1887.

» Nowodworski's Collegium was built in 1636-1643 according to the design of Jan Leitner.

« A monument portraying Nicholas Copernicus as a student of the Kraków Academy, where he studied in 1491-1495, was created by Cyprian Godebski and originally erected in the courtyard of Collegium Maius. In 1953, it was moved to the gardens of Witkowski's Collegium.

≫ Witkowski College, also known as Collegium Physicum, was erected in 1908-1911 on the site of the former gardens of Collegium Maius. This neo-Gothic building, incorporating neo-Romanesque and Art Nouveau elements, was the work of G. Niewiadomski.

⋩⋨» Collegium Maius is Poland's oldest university building, founded in 1400 by King Ladislaus II Jagiełło. Italian construction theories are reflected in the design of this late-Gothic edifice, believed to have been built by Master Jan of Cologne.

» A university library was built onto the south side of the Collegium Maius building in 1515-1540 by master builder Benedykt. A decorative stone portal known as Porta Aurea leads to premises whose ceilings display Gothic net vaulting and stellar-net vaulting.

⌃ On display at the Jagiellonian University museum are old scientific instruments, the oldest of which date from the 15th century.

⌃ At ceremonies, during which when honorary doctorates are conferred, members of the university senate occupy seats in the historic old stalls.

« A Baroque Gdańsk-style staircase is found in the chamber known as 'Stuba Communis'.

The originally Gothic Church of St Anne was remodelled in the Baroque style in honour of St John Cantius, a professor of the Kraków Academy. The renovation project according to the design of Tylman of Gameren got under way in 1689. The interior décor was created in 1695-1703 by Baltazar Fontana and painters Karol and Innocenty Montich.

« A figure of St Stanislaus at the side of the main altar.

≫ A pulpit created by Andrzej Frączkiewicz in 1720-1721.

≫ The Confession of St John Cantius, was created in 1695-1703 by Baltazar Fontana according to a drawing by Jerzy Eleuter Siemiginowski.

« ⌃ The Stary Theatre (No. 1 Jagiellońska Street) is Poland's oldest theatre building — a function it has fulfilled without interruption since 1798. In 1903-1905, the edifice was remodelled according to the design of Franciszek Mączyński and Tadeusz Stryjeński.

» The Art Nouveau-style Palace of Arts (No. 4 Szczepański Square) was built in 1898-1901 for the Society of Friends of Fine Arts.

≽» The Church of St Mark the Evangelist (No. 10 Świętego Marka Street) was founded in 1293 and acquired its present form in the 14th and 15th centuries.

≽ The Church of the Reformati (No. 4 Reformacka Street) was built in 1666-1672.

» The Baroque-style Church of St John (No. 7 Świętego Jana Street) has retained Romanesque and Gothic elements from its earlier predecessors.

☞ The Baroque-style palace of the Cistercian Abbots of Jędrzejów, situated at the corner of Świętego Marka and Świętego Jana Streets, was built in the early 1740s according to the design of Francesco Placidi.

« Early-classicist Wodzicki Palace (No. 11 Świętego Jana Street) was built in 1781-1789 presumably according to the design of Ferdinand Nax. The building is topped with an attic adorned with a cartouche bearing the Leliwa crest of the Wodzicki clan.

The early-Classicist Church of the Piarist Fathers (No. 2 Pijarska Street), which closes off Świętego Jana Street from the north, was built in 1718-1728 most likely according to the design of Kacper Bażanka. The splendid rococo façade, designed by Francesco Placidi, was added somewhat later in 1759-1761. Its interior is adorned with illusionist polychromy patterned on the mural paintings of Andrea del Pozza in Rome's Church of St Ignatius. It was the work of Franciszek Eckstein.

The Czartoryski Museum owes its existence to Izabela Czartoryska who created Poland's oldest collection of art works. Originally accumulated in Płock, the historic items were moved to Kraków in 1876 and stored in three dwelling houses in Świętego Jana Street, linked to what was known as 'the little monastery' (above) by above-road connectors (at left). The museum's collection boasts many outstanding works, the most valuable of which include Rembrandt's 'Landscape with the Good Samaritan' and Leonardo da Vinci's 'Lady with an Ermine' (at right).

≈ ≋ Mediaeval Kraków since the 14th century was surrounded by numerous defensive watchtowers in the form of low bay windows positioned at 40 to 50-metre intervals. In the 15th, 16th and 17th centuries they were built up into hexagonal or semicircular, mainly brick towers. Carpenter's Tower, Cabinet-maker's Tower (above) and Sash-maker's Tower (below) all date from the 15th century.

Florian Gate, first mentioned in 1307, defended access to the town from the most endangered northern approach. Originally a one-storey structure, in the 14th and 15th centuries it acquired its present form of a quadrangular tower. Its town side is adorned by

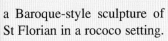
a Baroque-style sculpture of
St Florian in a rococo setting.

The Gothic-style Barbican, also known as 'the pot', was erected in 1489-1499 in conenction with the threat of a Valachian-Turkish invasion following King John Olbracht's defeat in Bukovina. It exemplifies the changes taking place in 15th-century defensive architecture as a result of the development of artillery. Originally surrounded by a 3.4-metre-deep moat, it was joined to Florian Gate by a long neck.

˥ Matejko House (No. 41 Floriańska Street) in 1838 was the birthplace of Poland's best-known painter. In 1872, the artist had the façade remodelled in the neo-Baroque style.

» Established in 1895, 'Jama Michalika' (Michalik's Cave) pastry shop (No. 45 Floriańska Street) was a favourite meeting place of artists and writers at the turn of the 20th century.

⩗ The Julisuz Słowacki Theatre (No. 1 Świętego Du-cha Square) was built in 1891-1893 on the site of a former hospital and monastery of the Holy Ghost Fathers. A competition for the best architectural design was won by Jan Zawieyski who gave the building a neo-Renaissance treatment.

» Many historic buildings have survived along Szpitalna Street.

≫ An Art Nouveau-style stained-glass window in one of the houses in Szpitalna Street.

≪ In 1900, a monument to the famous Polish comedy writer Aleksander Fredro was erected in front of the Słowacki Theatre. The marble bust was the work of Cyprian Godebski.

≫ At the back of the theatre stands an eclectic building of the former theatre power-plant. At present it houses the Słowacki Theatre's 'Miniatura' Stage.

≋ ≋ Construction of the Gothic-style Holy Cross Church
(No. 23 Świętego Krzyża
Street) for the Holy Ghost
Order was begun after 1300 at
the site of an earlier church. It
was at that time that the rectangular field-stone presbytery was built. In the first half
of the 14th century, the buildings hull and tower were
erected.

≫ The interior of Holy Cross Church contains many valuable architectural relics from different epochs. Among the most important are the Gothic baptistry dating from 1423 and a Renaissance-style triptych from the Węgrzyn Family Chapel.

« The Gothic vaulting displaying a complex ribbed design is supported by a slender, cylindrical pillar. The mural paintings date from before 1571.

≫ Planty, a green-belt park picturesquely encircling Kraków's historic old district, was laid out mainly in 1810-1814 on the site of the town's razed defensive walls.

≪ A monument to Queen Hedwig and King Ladislaus Jagiełło was erected at the exit of Sławkowskiej Street.

⌃ A monument to the well-known painter Artur Grottger was unveiled in 1903.

⌄ A monument to poet Józef Zaleski created by Pius Weloński.

⌄ Fountain in the Planty green belt.

STRADOM

Already in the early Middle Ages, a settlement situated to the south of Wawel Hill had been known as Stradom. From 1335, that settlement separated Kraków from the newly created town of Kazimierz. Its location in the Vistula's marshy flood-water area was not conducive to Stradom's development. It was not until 1655 that grand palaces and churches began being built there. Most of its dwelling houses date from the 19th century.

» The polychromy vaulting of the church of the missionary priests was created in 1862-1863 according to the design of Izydor Jabłoński.

≫ A scene depicting a cleric being tempted by Satan graces the elevation of Częstochowa Seminary (No. 3 Bernardyńska Street).

⋩» The emergence of the Bernardine Church and Monastery in Stradom (No. 2 Bernardyńska Street) was connected to a visit to Kraków in 1453 by the preacher St John of Capistrano. His fiery sermons inspired dozens of Kraków burghers to join the Bernardine Order and launch the church's construction. Destroyed during the 1655 Swedish invasion, the original Gothic structure was rebuilt in the Baroque style in 1659-1680. Its main altar dates from 1758-1766.

⤊⤋ The Baroque-style church (No. 4 Stradomska Street), belonging to missionary priests brought to Kraków in 1682, was built in 1719-1728 according to Kacper Bażanka's design, The church's architecture alludes to the works of outstanding Italian Baroque artists Gianlorenzo Bernini and Pietro of Cortona. Its Baroque interior was additionally illuminated by mirrors adorning its walls.

» Hotel Saski

KAZIMIERZ

The town of Kazimierz, founded by King Casimir the Great who granted it a municipal charter in 1335, rose up round the settlements surrounding the churches of St Michael on the Rock, St James and St Lawrence. Surrounded by arms of the Vistula, it had its own marketplace and town hall. Towards the end of the 15th century during the reign of John Olbracht, the Jews of Kraków were resettled in a specially mapped out quarter of Kazimierz.

» A restaurant in the old Jewish quarter.

≽ A typical Jewish candlestick from the museum housed in an old synagogue.

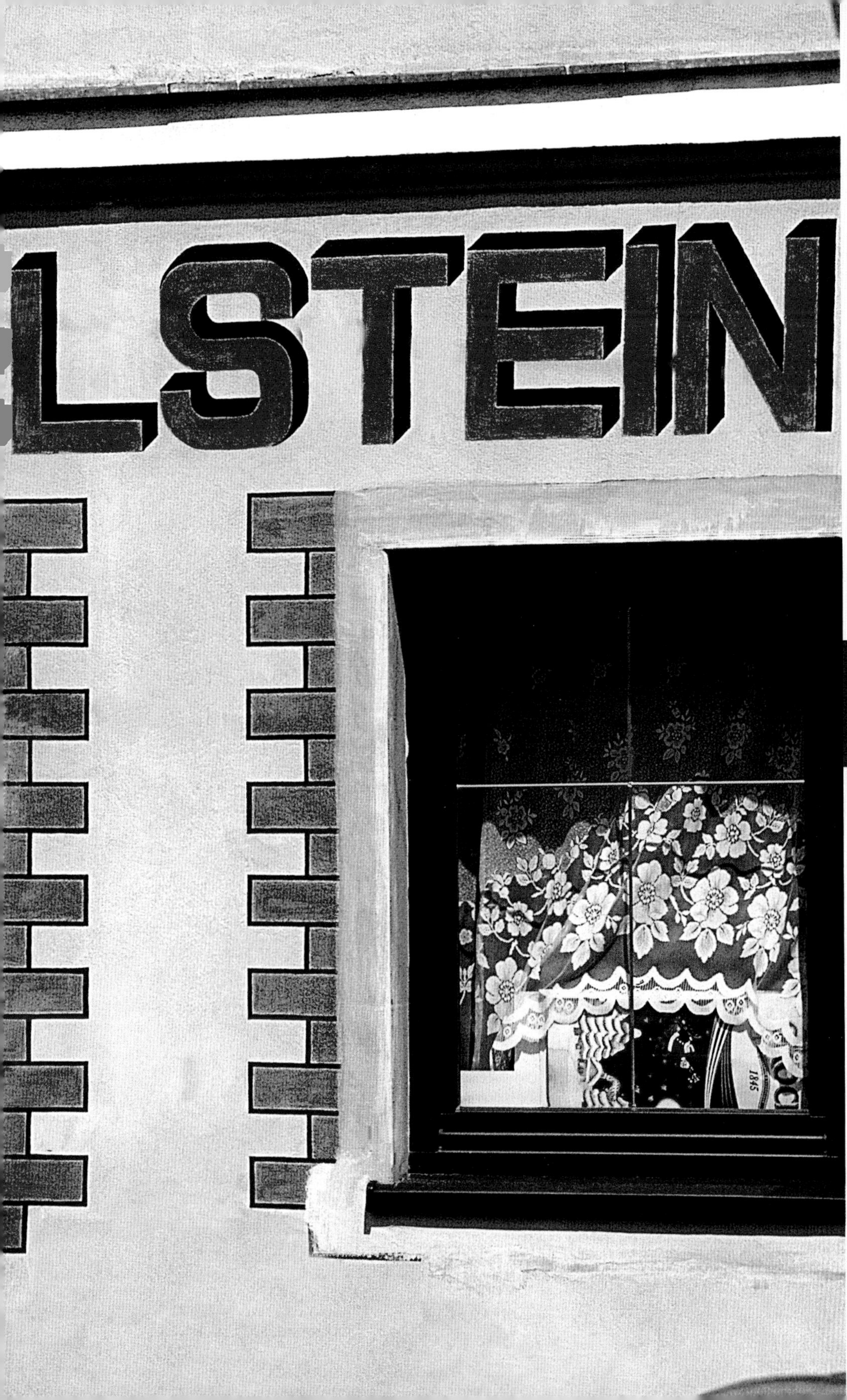
LSTEIN
1845

≽ Krakowska Street was already in existence in 1385 as the axis of the town of Kazimierz, linking the Clay Gate and Salt Gate with the marketplace. Although of earlier vintage, the dwelling houses date from the 19th century and stand out for their interesting architectural details.

« A belfry erected next to St Catherine's Church in the 15th century.

» A covered porch, built in 1728, joins St Catherine's Church to the Augustinian Sisters' Convent.

« ⌃ According to chronicler John Długosz, St Catherine's Church (No. 7 Augustiańska Street) was founded by King Casimir the Great as an act of penance for murdering Father Marcin Baryczka. Construction of the Gothic-style church is believed to have begun in 1343 and continued on into the early 16th century.

⌃ A neo-rococo gate with a decorative grate designed by Karol Knaus leads to Skałka (the Rock).

«⌃ The place known today as Skałka was connected to the tragic death of St Stanislaus at the hands of Boleslaus the Bold in 1079. A Romanesque rotunda most probably already existing at the site in the 11th century was remodelled in the Gothic style in the 14th century. After the church was dismantled in 1733, construction of a new Baroque-style church designed by Antoni Müntzer got under way.

« In the basement of the church at Skałka is the Crypt of Honour, a national pantheon of people who had made important contributions to Polish culture. In 1880, John Długosz was reinterred there on the 400th anniversary of his death. Later, other outstanding Poles were laid to rest there including poet Wincenty Pol, poet and playwright Stanisław Wyspiański, painter Jacek Malczewski and most recently poet Czesław Miłosz.

⌃ The pulpit's decoration was the work of Wojciech Rojewski.

The décor of the basilica-type interior of the Church of St Michael the Archangel and St Stanislaus at Skałka (No. 15 Skałeczna Street) dates from the 18th century. Its Baroque-style altar contains a picture of Michael the Archangel, painted by Tadeusz Kontze-Konicz in 1758. The stucco decorations were created by Jan Jerzy Lechert.

« The late-Baroque Church of the Hospitaller Brothers (No. 48 Krakowska Street), erected in 1741-1758 by Francesco Placidi, enthrals beholders with its superb, wavy façade.

⩘ ⩗ The Kazimierz town hall in its Renaissance form dates from 1623. It now houses an Ethnographic Museum.

87

⌃ This late-Baroque pulpit in the shape of a ship, supported by mermaids and dolphins, was created before 1749.

Gothic-style Corpus Christi parish church (No. 25 Bożego Ciała Street), founded by King Casimir the Great, was built at the spot where thieves abandoned a monstrance with a host stolen from All Saints Church. The building project lasted from 1340 until the mid-15th century. Master builders from the Czipser family were involved in the construction. The church's interior is an excellent example of Baroque-style woodwork of the 17th and 18th centuries.

A JEWISH TOWN

Jewish inhabitants were already documented in Kazimierz in 1485, but the emergence of a separate Jewish town dates from 1495. It was then, after a fire in the capital, that King John Olbracht ordered Jews to leave Kraków and settle in Kazimierz in a ghetto surrounded by a wall.

《≈ The neo-Romanesque Tempel Synagogue (No. 24 Miodowa Street) arose in 1860-1862 and is one of two functioning synagogues in Kazimierz. Rich appointments have survived in its interior.

« Kup's Synagogue (No. 8 J. Warszauera Street) was built in the first half of the 17th century to serve as a hospital for the poor. It was remodelled in 1830-1834.

» The Old Synagogue (No. 24 Szeroka Street), dating from the turn of the 16th century, is the oldest preserved synagogue in Kraków. An antechamber once led into the synagogue.

≫ The High Synagogue (No. 38 Józefa Street), built in 1556-1563, owes its name to the hall of prayer situated on the first floor. A rich late-Renaissance portal adorns its exterior wall.

≈ The Baroque-style Synagogue of Isaac (No. 22 Jakuba Street) was built in 1638-1644.

≫ » The interior of the Old Synagogue, supported by two columns, today houses the Judaism collection of the Kraków Historical Museum.

≽ Period restaurants along Szeroka Street.

» An obelisk dedicated to 30 Poles killed by the Nazis at this spot on 1943.

≽ » The Remuh Synagogue (No. 40 Szeroka Street), founded in 1553, serves orthodox Jews to this day. Its interior includes a decorative pulpit and Baroque-style altar case.

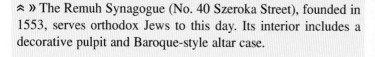

≈ ≈ Poland's oldest Jewish cemetery (kirkut), in which Jews were buried from the latter half of the 16th century, adjoins the Remuh synagogue. Uniquely symbolic Renaissance-style tombstones and a Wailing Wall (below) have survived.

PODGÓRZE

Podgórze was a town established on the right bank of the Vistula by Emperor Josef II in 1784 to compete with Kraków. After the first partition of Poland in 1776 that area was occupied by Austria. In 1915, Podgórze was incorporated into Kraków.

» The buildings of Podgórze mostly date from the 19th century.

≽ Stag House in Podgórze at No. 12 Marketplace dates from the end of the 18th century. In the 19th century a superb hotel flourished there.

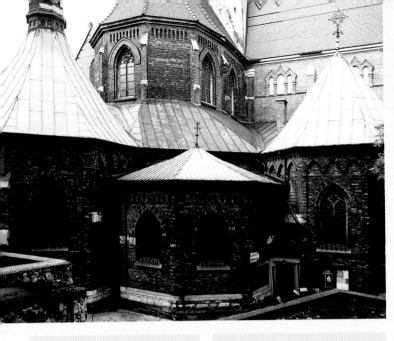

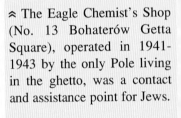

≫ St Joseph's Church was built in the Podgórze Marketplace in 1909 according to the architectural design of Jan Sas Zubrzycki.

≫ The town hall was built in 1844-1845 in the style of late historicism.

≫ The Eagle Chemist's Shop (No. 13 Bohaterów Getta Square), operated in 1941-1943 by the only Pole living in the ghetto, was a contact and assistance point for Jews.

≫ Fort St Benedict is a remnant of former Austrian fortifications.

≈ St Benedict's Church, situated at the edge of Lassota's Hill, encloses within its walls a Romanesque 'palatium' cum rotunda dating from c. 1000. The church was thoroughly remodelled towards the close of the 16th century.

≈ Krak's Mound is the legendary burial place of King Krak. It is believed to have been created in the 7th-8th centuries round a wooden post surrounded by radiating wicker walls.

KLEPARZ, WESOŁA AND BISKUPIE

Over the centuries, numerous settlements arose around Kraków and became independent municipal organisms. The nearest was Kleparz, which received a municipal charter from King Casimir the Great in 1366. Over time, private towns known as jurisdictions, which constituted independent economic organisms, rose up around Kleparz. These included Wesoła to the east and Biskupie, Błonie and Pędzichów to the west.

» Opposite the Barbican is Matejko Square, which together with the Kleparz marketplace constitutes the town centre of today's Kleparz.

≫ St Joseph's altar in the Jesuit Church in Kopernika Street.

98

≋» The building of the Medical Society (No. 4 Radziwiłłowska Street) was built in 1904. Its interior contains a stained-glass window 'Apollo - solar system' designed by Stanisław Wyspiański.

≋ The Church of St Nicholas is one of Kraków's oldest places of worship and dates from the Romanesque period. Its present Baroque appearance dates from 1677-1682.

« The Church and Monastery of the Discalced Carmelites (No. 44 Kopernika Street) was built in 1720-1732. The Baroque-style church, built on the plan of a Greek cross, stands out for its superb façade.

The Jesuit Church (No. 36 Kopernika Street) was built in 1909-1921 according to the design of Franciszek Mączyński. The combination of various historical styles has contributed to an outstanding architectural work. Distinguished artists led by Karol Hukan, Xawery Dunikowski and Piotr Stachiwewicz worked on the church's interior décor.

≽ The Main Railway Station was built in the neo-Gothic style according to the design of architect Piotr Rosenbaum. The building's neo-Gothic trappings were removed during a renovation in 1910.

« The building of the National Bank of Poland (No. 20 Basztowa Street) was built in 1921-1925 in a style alluding to classicist forms.

» The Polish state Railways building (No. 12 Matejko square), built in 1888 by an unknown Austrian architect, combines neo-Renaissance and neo-Baroque elements.

« The Monument of King Ladislaus Jagiełło, known as the Grunwald Monument, was erected in 1910 to mark the 500th anniversary of the Battle of Grunwald. It was founded by the composer and pianist, Ignacy Jan Paderewski.

≋ ↘ » St Florian's Church (No. 1 Warszawska Street) was built at the spot where, according to legend, the wagons bringing St Florian's relics to Kraków came to a stop. The original church was built there in 1185-1216. It acquired its present Baroque appearance in 1677-1684.

≫ The Church of St Vincent de Paul (No. 19 Świętego Filipa Street) was built in 1876-1877 in a style alluding to Italian Romanesque.

≫ The Church of the Sisters of Charity (No. 8 Warszawska Street) was built by Filip Pokutyński in the years 1869-1871.

≫ The Baroque-style Church of the Visitation Sisters (ul. Krowoderska 16) was built in 1685-95 according to the design of Giovanni Solari.

≫ » The Art Nouveau-style Globe House (No. 1 Długa Street) was built according to the design of Franciszek Mączyński and Tadeusz Stryjeński in 1904-1906. Paintings by Józef Mehofer grace its interior.

PIASEK AND NOWY ŚWIAT

Some time after 1363, leather-tanners settled to the west of Kraków, just beyond Shoemaker's Gate, hence the name of their settlement Garbary. The name was not changed to Piasek (sand) until the 19th century. Before Vistula Gate, to the south of Piasek, were many privately owned towns which were jointly incorporated into Kraków in 1800 under the name of Nowy Świat (New World).

» The high street of Piasek is Karmelicka Street with its 19th-century architecture.

≽ An original mascaron from Hutten-Czapski Palace.

≈ Spider House (No. 35 Karmelicka Street) was the outstanding 1889 work of architect Teodor Talowski.

» The neo-Romanesque Church and Convent of the Sacred Heart Sisters (No. 26 Garncarska Street) were built in 1895-1900 according to the design of Władysław Kaczmarski.

≈ ٦ » The Baroque-style Carmelite Church (No. 19 Karmelicka Street) was build before 1679 on the fire-gutted remains of an earlier house of worship. A late-Baroque Calvary is seen on its side elevation.

≫ The building of the Union of Industrial and Craft Youth (No. 2-4 Skarbowa Street) dates from 1930.

≫ Neo-Renaissance Hutten-Czapski Palace dating from 1884.

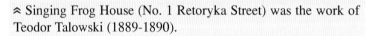

≫ Singing Frog House (No. 1 Retoryka Street) was the work of Teodor Talowski (1889-1890).

≫ The filial of the Art Nouveau-style dwelling house at No. 30 Piłsudskiego Street.

» The building of the Kraków Philharmonic (No. 1 Zwierzyniecka Street) was built in 1928-1930.

« The Stanisław Wyspiański monument standing in front of the National Museum was designed by Marian Konieczny and erected n 1982.

⚞ The building of the 'Sokół' (Falcon) Gymnastic Society (No. 27 Piłsudskiego Street) was erected in 1889.

111

ANOTHER QUARTERS

Over the centuries, numerous settlements grew up around Kraków and developed along with the capital, but they often were administratively independent. In the 19th and 20th centuries, those localities were incorporated into Kraków. They included Zwierzyniec, Bielany, Bronowice and Mogiła. A totally new Kraków district is Nowa Huta, whose construction got under way in 1949 together with the creation of a giant steel-making complex.

» A park on St Bronislava's Hill where the Kościuszuko Mound is located.

≽ On the octave of Corpus Christi, the court-yard of the Norbertine Sisters' Convent is the starting point of a colourful Tartar Hobby-horse Parade, whose tradition goes back to the 1287 Tartar invasion.

≫ The Church of SS Augustine and John the Baptist and the Norbertine Convent in Zwierzyniec, dating from the 12th century, acquired their present architectural form in the first half of the 17th century.

« The Church of the Most Holy Saviour in Zwierzyniec is regarded as one of Kraków's oldest. Believed to have been erected round the turn of the 12th century, it was partially rebuilt in the Baroque style in the 17th century.

» The Kościuszko Mound was built in 1820-1823 to commemorate the leader of the 1794 insurrection. At the foot of the mound is the Chapel of Blessed Bronislava whose hermit's hut was said to have been situated there.

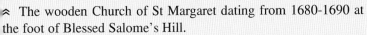
⤒ The wooden Church of St Margaret dating from 1680-1690 at the foot of Blessed Salome's Hill.

⤒ In 1846-1848, after the Free City of Kraków had been incorporated into Austria, the Austrians set about building fortifications, portions of which have survived down to the present.

«≽ The Camedulian Church and Monastery was built between 1604 and 1630 on Srebrna Góra (Silver Hill) in Bielany, a place ideally suited to this particular religious order, whose hermit monks live in huts isolated from the world. Except for 12 specific feastdays in the year, women are strictly forbidden to enter the monastery grounds. The church with its mannerist façade, designed by Andrea Spezza, has largely Baroque-style interior appointments.

≈ ≈ The Benedictine Tyniec Abbey was built on a tall, rocky bluff overlooking the Vistula in the latter half of the 11th century. In the 15th century, a Gothic church and monastery were built on the ruins of the earlier Romanesque structure. In the early 17th century, these were remodelled in the Baroque style.

≽ Wolski Forest is the biggest forest complex in Kraków, a portion of which has been turned into a park.

» The Renaissance-style Decjusz Villa (No. 1 Kasztanowa Street) was built in the 1530s according to a design by Bartolomeo Berrecci and Giovanni Cini.

↙↖ Rydlówka Manor in Bronowice Małe was the scene of Lucjan Rydel's and Jadwiga Mikołajczyk's wedding feast, immortalised by Stanisław Wyspiański in his play 'The Wedding'.

» Rakowicki Cemetery in Kraków's north end, the city's biggest burial ground, dates from 1801.

≈ » The Lord's Ark Church in Bieńczyce was built in 1967-1977 according to Wojciech Pietrzak's design, patterned on Le Corbusier Chapel in Ronchamp.

≈ The manor house in Krzesławice was purchased by painter Jan Matejko in 1876. The artist lived there until his death in 1893.

⋠ The wooden Church of St Bartholomew in Mogiła, dating from the early 13th century, was built in 1466. Its Gothic portal reveals the carved name of Maciej Mączka who most likely built the church.

⇖⋩ The Cistercian Church and Monastery in Mogiła were built in 1220-1266 but acquired their Baroque appearance during a renovation in 1780-1790.

SURROUNDINGS

» To the north-west of Kraków lies a scenic park known as 'Dolinki Krakowskie' (Little Kraków Valleys). One of its most picturesque areas is Dolina Będkowska.

≪ South-west of Kraków is Kalwaria Zebrzydowska containing a complex of chapels commemorating the Passion and Death of Jesus.

» Bat Cave in the 'Dolinki Krakowskie' park was inhabited by homo sapiens 38,000 years ago.

« Only ruins have remained of Ojców Castle, built by Casimir the Great.

≳ A wooden Chapel on the Water stands in Ojców on the bank of the River Prądnik on the site of former spa baths.

≳ Pieskowa Skała Castle in the Prądnik Valley was built in the 14th century by Casimir the Great. In 1542-1544, the Szafraniec family had it remodelled in the Renaissance style to resemble Wawel Castle. The renovation was carried out by Italian architect Nicola Castiglione.

» Ojców National Park encompasses the picturesque Prądnik and Sąspówka valleys, cut deeply into Jurassic rock. The area is known for its fantastic rock formations having the shape of needles, towers, gates and clubs (at left: the well-known Hercules' Club) as well as caverns.

≽ Picturesque Dolina Będkowska north-west of Kraków.

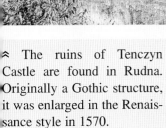

≽ The neo-classicist palace in Krzeszowice was built for Adam Potocki in 1850 according to the design of Francesco Maria Lanci.

≽ The ruins of Tenczyn Castle are found in Rudna. Originally a Gothic structure, it was enlarged in the Renaissance style in 1570.

» The Baroque-style Monastery of the Discalced Carmelites in Czerna was founded by Agnieszka Tęczyńska in 1631-1640.

↳ « ≫ The shrine at Kalwaria Zebrzydowska was founded in 1600 by Mikołaj Zebrzydowski on Żarek Hill. Next to the church and Bernardine monastery, Poland's biggest Calvary was created comprising chapels and shrines scattered about the surrounding hilly terrain.

≫ Niepolomice Castle was built at the behest of Casimir the Great in the mid-14th century. In 1550-1571, it was remodelled into a Renaissance-style royal hunting residence with a quadrangular courtyard. In 1637, the courtyard was enclosed by stone galleries.

≪≫ The salt-mine in Wieliczka has been included on UNESCO's World Cultural Heriatge List. Its oldest shaft dates from 1280. Many of the chambers have been adorned with rock-salt sculptures.

« A classicist palace was built in Igołomia to the east of Krakow in the 18th and 19th centuries. Its park contains an exhibition of archaeological excavations conducted in the area.

≫ » An historic park and manor complex including a 1603 Renaissance storehouse and an early-19th century manor house is found in Branice.